SYMBOLISM AND

ASTROLOGY:

AN INTRODUCTION TO ESOTERIC ASTROLOGY

SYMBOLISM AND ASTROLOGY:

AN INTRODUCTION TO ESOTERIC ASTROLOGY

ALAN LEO

COSIMO CLASSICS

NEW YORK

Library of Congress Cataloging-in-Publication Data
A catalog record for this book is available from the Library of Congress

Cover design by www.wiselephant.com

ISBN: 1-59605-614-2

PREFACE

THE interest in Astrology is now spreading so rapidly that it is attracting the attention of many who find themselves at a loss to know where to begin this study, and who require an easy introduction to a science which embraces so much.

It is for those who have made no previous study of the subject that this Manual, the first of a new series, has been written. The aim of the author has been to make the whole subject elementary, and through an explanation of three pure symbols he has introduced elaborations embracing the major portion of the symbolism of Astrology.

ALAN LEO.

Imperial Buildings,
    Ludgate Circus, E.C.
        1914.

In this New Series of manuals an attempt will be made to bring out the inner and deeper meaning of the subject, particularly with regard to Natal Astrology.

ASTROLOGY

THE word literally means a knowledge of the stars, a discourse concerning the stars, or the science of the stars. Aster, star; logos, reason.

Astrology is not only a science, it is a philosophy and to some a religion. It has many branches and may be studied under seven of these to advantage.

(1) ASTRO-METEOROLOGY, the study of the influence of the heavenly bodies upon weather changes, storms and earthquakes.

(2) MUNDANE ASTROLOGY, also called National, State, or Civic Astrology, which studies the influence of New Moons, Eclipses, Ingresses, Planetary Conjunctions and Comets upon the fate of nations, countries and peoples.

(3) HORARY ASTROLOGY, the answering of questions and the solving of doubts arising in the mind upon any subject from a study of a map of the heavens for the moment when the question is asked.

(4) GENETHLIACAL OR NATAL ASTROLOGY, the science of the influence of the heavenly bodies upon the individual man, based upon his horoscope of birth.

(5) MEDICAL ASTROLOGY, the relation of planetary influence to bodily health and disease.

(6) ESOTERIC ASTROLOGY, the more religious and philosophical side of the subject, generally studied now-a-days in the light of the law of Karma and the evolution of the soul through reincarnation.

(7) OCCULT ASTROLOGY deals with the higher mysteries and with the bearing of Astrology upon practical occultism.

Originally Astrology and Astronomy were synonymous terms, but to-day they are separated in the minds of many; there is, however, a tendency at the beginning of the twentieth century to regard as probable the belief that Astrology is the soul of Astronomy.

Astrology is the science that investigates the action and reaction constantly going on between the celestial bodies and the rest of manifested nature, including man, and reveals the laws under which this takes place. Its antiquity is such as to place it among the very earliest records of human learning. It was for long ages a secret science in the East, and in its final expression remains so to this day.

CONTENTS.

CHAPTER I.

The Simplicity of Astrology

GREAT truths are often hidden in simple statements, and we frequently travel far only to discover that we have missed the spirit of truth that is to be found at our own doors concealed in simple ideas.

To the uninitiated, the science or art of Astrology appears complicated and its study too intricate to be followed or understood easily ; this notion, however, is erroneous and is mainly caused by confusion of thought and the misconceptions which bias or prejudice has introduced into the subject.

The simplicity of Astrology begins with its unique symbology, for out of the three plain symbols of Circle, Cross and Semi-circle, most of the elaborations of its symbolical language have arisen.

The circle symbolises both the centre and the circumference of the Solar System.

The circle with the point in the centre is the universal symbol of the Sun. In all ages, by all nations, and in every part of the globe, it has been the symbol for the Supreme Intelligence, the

Logos of the System; and Sabeanism or Sun Worship in one or another of its forms is consequently the oldest religion in the world.

To the Sun Worshippers the Sun was the outer symbol of the central Sun and represented the glorious garment or body of the God of the Solar System.

Spirit, life, consciousness, energy, all are symbolised as springing from the point in the centre of the circle; the circumference signifying the boundary line of space within the Solar universe.

The semi-circle is the circle divided into two separate halves that are above and below the horizon, and are the light and the dark. It is the symbol of the Moon and represents the Soul in man, that which is neither wholly spiritual nor wholly material, but partakes of the nature of both and is the connecting link between the spirit and the physical body.

The cross is but a continuation of the point in the centre of the circle; it divides the circle into the four primary quarters of East, West, North and South, and represents all definite-. ness of form or limitation, such as birth, life periods of varying lengths, death or change of form and the moulding of forms that are coming into manifestation.

☉	Sun or Circle	— Spirit, Life, Consciousness.
☽	Moon or Semi-circle	— Soul, Breath, Instinct.
+	Earth or Cross	— Body, Matter, Concretions.

The symbols of the planets, the aspects between the planets and the various states of matter or ether, represented by the zodiac, are all depicted by these three plain symbols in various combinations, as will be seen in the chapters following ; but however complicated the symbols become, they have all their origin in the three great truths that underlie them.

(1) THE SUN is a symbol of the essence of Life in all its various phases of manifestation, whether spiritual or physical ; and everything that lives and moves partakes of this Solar Life. It also represents the Life of God, " in whom we live and move and have our being," and suggests the immanence of God and the promise of immortality.

It symbolises the highest and the purest metal, Gold, an emblem of perfection upon the terrestrial plane, as the Sun is the symbol of perfection in the superterrestrial plane ; in colour Orange, and in sound the note *Re ;* of precious stones it symbolises the diamond, of days in the week Sunday, and of numbers 1 and 10.

(2) THE MOON symbolises the most subtle forms of matter, the fine film of substance around the physical body of man known as the etheric double, or the mould upon which physical man is formed, and corresponds to matter that is vaporous, volatile and constantly changing. It is the reflection of the Real, or its Shadow. It represents the colour Violet, and in sound the note *Si ;*

the day of the week it governs is Monday, and of precious stones the Opal and Amethyst. Its metal is Silver, an emblem of Intelligence, symbolised by the Moon. Amalgamated with Mercury (the mind) and penetrated by the Fire of the divine Love, it becomes transformed into the Gold of wisdom.

(3)   The equal armed CROSS symbolises manifestation in all its varied forms; it is an ever-changing symbol out of which all possible geometrical figures may be formed.

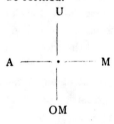

The Cross is a symbol expressing various ideas, but especially the creative power of Life in a spiritual aspect, acting within the Macrocosm of nature and the Microcosm of man.   It also represents Spirit and Matter ascending and descending.   The perpendicular beam represents Spirit, the horizontal bar the animal or earthly principle being penetrated by the divine Spirit.   Universal as well as individual man may be symbolised by a Cross. Man's animal body is a Cross, or instrument of torture for the soul.   By means of his battle with the lower elements of his constitution, his divine nature becomes developed.   By means of his physical body, man is nailed to the cross of suffering appertaining to terrestrial existence.   The animal elements are to die upon that

Cross, and the spiritual man is to be resurrected to become united with the Christ. "Death upon the Cross" represents the giving up of one's own personality and the entering into eternal and universal life. The inscription sometimes found at the top of the Cross, consisting of the letters I.N.R.I., means, in its esoteric sense, *Igne Natura Renovata Integra;* that is to say by the (divine) Fire (of Love) all Nature becomes renewed. The golden Cross represents spiritual Life, illuminated by Wisdom. It is the symbol of immortality.

In a cosmic sense, these three symbols represent Will ☉, Wisdom ☽, and Activity +.

The ☉ may also be regarded as representing the Self, the + the Not-Self, and the ☽ the relation between the two.

In the highest form of symbolism these three represent the Trinity in all its various modes of expression, and in the religions that use these symbols they are the Father, Mother, Child.

CHAPTER II.

The Cross and the Earth

THE revolution of the earth on its own axis, once in every twenty-four hours, forms a distinct Cross, marking four definite points in time; they are :—

SUNRISE, when the Sun appears to rise upon the eastern horizon, causing the break of day and symbolising Birth.

NOON, when the Sun appears to be upon the upper meridian, illuminating one half of the earth's surface and symbolising Life, Maturity and Vitality.

SUNSET, when the Sun sinks into the West and causes twilight, evening and semi-darkness, and symbolising Death, Decay and the End.

MIDNIGHT, when there is *complete* darkness, or the absence of light from the Sun. This corresponds to deep sleep or the negation of physical and external activity, and symbolises Immortality, Nirvana and the *non-reflection* of light.

In the physical body of man we find a strange corres-

6

pondence to the earth and its diurnal revolution. There is a striking similarity between sunrise and youth. The physical body is born out of darkness into light, it grows amazingly fast, gaining strength and vigour from Birth to Youth, just as the Sun becomes more powerful between Sunrise and Noon.

There is again a singular resemblance between Noon when the Sun is on the Meridian, and the maturity of the body, when it is filled with life and power.

At Sunset, we find another remarkable agreement between the Sun's setting with diminished light, and the sinking of the body into the sleep of death and decay, or the *body's* ending.

By Midnight, all that remained of the light of the Sun has entirely vanished, and we are taught that finally all traces of man's vestures disappear when he enters the glorious mansion of the Father in Heaven.

Diagram I. illustrates the correspondence that exists between the earth and man's physical body ; it is the ground-plan of the hour-scope or horoscope, out of which all the elaborate complications arise connected with man's destiny or the events affecting the physical body.

Critical planetary positions affecting the Ascendant, threaten the body and assist in terminating its existence ; hence the importance to be attached to planets rising.

The maturity of life, represented by the Mid-heaven, also affected by the condition of the planets near the

THE CROSS OR SKELETON HOROSCOPE

LIFE

Maturity
Noon
M.C. or Meridian

BIRTH	The Eastern Horizon	The Western Angle	DEATH
Sunrise	or Ascendant	or Descendant	*Sunset*

Nadir
Midnight
Rest
IMMORTALITY

DIAGRAM I.

mid-heaven at birth, and everything connected with
avocation, honour and reputation is denoted by it.

The unions or partnerships, which mean the *sharing*
of the physical conditions with another, are represented
by the Descendant.

The psychic and subconscious conditions are represented by the Nadir, and the unseen conditions or home
life are denoted by it in all astrological judgments.

The Cross is the symbol of action, and also of the
bodily and physical activities in human affairs. The earth
is in constant motion, and ever forming fresh relations
with other bodies that are floating in the ether of space.
The physical body is also constantly changing not only
its physical particles, but also its relationship toward
other bodies.

The Cross is the symbol of expression, and the nearer
to its angles any planet is placed the more active and
expressive does it become.

It is upon the Cross, the earth's matter or the
physical body, that the life or consciousness of man is
crucified, and the greatest tragedy known to the world
was the Crucifixion, when the Son of God descended
into the Hell of the world to save sinners.

Upon the Cross the Sun or Son is eternally crucified,
and by that sublime crucifixion all men have tasted of
life and known the meaning of a separate and self-
conscious existence. Without the Cross, the earth, and

the body there could be no manifestation of Spirit;
hence the extreme importance of the Cross as a means
of self-realisation, and the value of a horoscope in
showing conditions of manifestation at the birth of an
individual.

CHAPTER III.

THE SEMI-CIRCLE AND THE SOUL

THE Soul is a fine film of substance, through which the divine Spirit is moving, as in a cup or vessel. It is the semi-material principle connecting matter with spirit. It leads, so to say, an amphibious existence between these two poles of substance, and may ultimately become amalgamated either with the one or the other. The Body is the mask of the Soul; the Soul the body of the Spirit.

It has three distinct phases of activity and one of latency or complete inertia, corresponding to the four phases of the Moon.

These phases of the soul are as actual as those of the Moon in the heavens, and they correspond to what are termed the Spiritual, Human and Animal Soul and the ' death ' of the Soul.

The half circle or semi-circle symbolises the Moon, which passes through the four distinct phases of New Moon, first quarter, full, third quarter, and finally New Moon once again.

11

The Moon in Astrology is the collector and receiver of all planetary vibrations, transmitting them to the human brain, which translates these vibrations into *influences* according to the temperament, surroundings and educational limits.

The Moon rises, culminates, and sets upon the cross of the horoscope, and in the course of the earth's daily revolution the Moon appears to be carried completely round the circle. The Moon in one month, or mooneth, travels through all the twelve signs of the zodiac, and during her journey round the zodiacal circle she transmits the influence of each sign in turn, taking about two and a half days to pass through a sign.

The Moon has close affinity with some of the zodiacal signs, whereas with others she is less receptive and responsive.

The zodiacal signs representing Earth and Water are more agreeable to her nature than those representing Fire and Air.

The Moon is also more receptive to certain planetary vibrations than to others. She responds readily to the planets Saturn, Mercury and Jupiter, but much less so to Mars, Venus and Uranus. To Neptune she is neutral.

The Moon again is more receptive in certain regions of the Cross than in others. She is more potent when below the horizontal line than when above; her influence below the earth being more in keeping with her mission to shine by night as a reflector of the Sun than by day when the Sun is visible.

The Moon is the intermediary between the planets and the earth, just as man's soul may be said to be intermediate between the spirit and the body.

The importance of the Moon as a factor in transmitting planetary influences is very great. She darkens and also brings to light the influence of the zodiac and the planets. She has a very close correspondence to the fluctuating soul moods of men and women; hence the necessity of understanding her influence in every nativity.

The Moon is a symbol of duality; she represents the formative principle in Nature and the limitations of the personal self through the instincts, sensations and moods or feelings.

The Moon is a very important factor in all astrological deductions, and her place at the moment of conception will decide the moment of birth and the sign rising upon the eastern horizon at that time.

As the right side of the body is positive and electric, while the left side is negative and magnetic, these two form a battery through which currents of electricity may freely pass. But, as was said in a previous work, even a short epitome of the Moon would fill a whole volume.

In all astrological judgments from an esoteric basis the Moon represents the Personality or the Mask; the sum and substance of the attributes which go to distinguish one man from others. As one and the same actor may appear in various costumes and masks, likewise one individual spiritual entity may appear successively on the stage of life in various personalities.

To comprehend the doctrine of Re-incarnation it should be remembered that at, and after, the transformation called 'death' only those attributes of a person which have reached a certain degree of spirituality, and are therefore fit to survive, will remain with the individual type. When the individuality again over-shadows a new-born form, it develops a new set of attributes, which go to make up its new personality.

CHAPTER IV.

Zodiacal Symbology

AROUND every manifesting form there is a circle of life ; around the earth there is an atmosphere charged with the vitalising rays of the Sun ; and around each man there is an aura filled with human life.

The earth's aura or limiting circle is the belt of its zodiac, and in this circle there are divisions having peculiar qualities known to the ancient philosophers as the essentials of Fire, Earth, Air and Water, symbolised as $\triangle \; \square = \triangledown$

Each of these divisions represents a quarter of the circle and contains three signs of the zodiac, classified as triplicities. The FIERY triplicity contains the signs, Aries (1), Leo (5), and Sagittarius (9). The EARTHY contains Taurus (2), Virgo (6), and Capricorn (10). The AIRY contains Gemini (3), Libra (7), and Aquarius (11). The WATERY contains Cancer (4), Scorpio (8), and Pisces (12). The ancient astrologers named the majority of these signs after certain animals in the following manner :—

Fire : Aries, the Ram ; Leo, the Lion ; Sagittarius the Archer on Horseback.

Earth : Taurus, the Bull ; Virgo, the Virgin ; Capricorn the Goat.

Air : Gemini, the Twins ; Libra, the Scales ; Aquarius, the Man.

Water : Cancer, the Crab ; Scorpio, the Scorpion ; Pisces, the Fish.

Each of these signs has its own peculiar symbol, which has been handed down to us from remote antiquity, very little variation being made in the signs by the many nations who have studied the zodiac. Some of these symbols are abbreviations of a whole symbol, such as the horns only of the Ram and the Bull. Others are not so clear, and are more difficult to explain ; yet each has a definite meaning. The symbols of the signs are as follows :—

FIRE	♈ ♌ ♐	*Aries, Leo, Sagittarius*
EARTH	♉ ♍ ♑	*Taurus, Virgo, Capricorn*
AIR	♊ ♎ ♒	*Gemini, Libra, Aquarius*
WATER	♋ ♏ ♓	*Cancer, Scorpio, Pisces*

The simplest method by which the symbols of the zodiacal signs may be understood is by knowing the parts of the body over which they have been definitely proved to rule. The arrangement as handed down through the ages is so perfect that alteration is now impossible, and it is as follows :—

Symbol	Sign	Ruling	Quality	Elements
♈	ARIES	Head	Cardinal	*Fire*
♉	TAURUS	Throat	Fixed	*Earth*
♊	GEMINI	Chest	Mutable	*Air*
♋	CANCER	Stomach	Cardinal	*Water*
♌	LEO	Heart	Fixed	*Fire*
♍	VIRGO	Bowels	Mutable	*Earth*
♎	LIBRA	Loins	Cardinal	*Air*
♏	SCORPIO	Secrets	Fixed	*Water*
♐	SAGITTARIUS	Thighs	Mutable	*Fire*
♑	CAPRICORN	Knees	Cardinal	*Earth*
♒	AQUARIUS	Ankles	Fixed	*Air*
♓	PISCES	Feet	Mutable	*Water*

As rulers over various parts of the human body, the signs of the zodiac are clearly related to the formative side of existence. From an esoteric standpoint they represent the various grades of matter or states of ether, and correspond to the substances necessary to express certain activities of human manifestation. The FIERY signs represent the substance through which mental states are expressed, and beginning with the head and the brain, the fiery sign Aries leads the zodiacal circle. The EARTHY signs are concerned with a more concrete substance through which physical expression takes the form of vital action expressed by Taurus, the leading sign of the earthy triplicity. The throat is the organ of voice production, from which follows the power of speech and song. The AIRY triplicity is concerned with a combination of the mental with the physical, a

B

dual expression, of which the mutable sign Gemini is the leading sign. Breathing and the lungs are the joint expression of the airy sign Gemini, which sign has also rule over the shoulders, arms and hands. Mind and action work more or less skilfully through the hands. The WATERY signs are concerned with the feelings and the expression of all sensation, and govern the fluidic state. They are led by Cancer, the Cardinal sign of the watery triplicity.

The primary or vital influences of the triplicities of signs may be classified as follows :—

Fiery signs govern the vitality, the magnetism and mental tone of the human form.

Earthy signs govern the stability, firmness and moral tone.

Airy signs govern the respiration, aspiration, intuition and responsive tone or elasticity of the form.

Watery signs govern the fluidic, soluble and sensitive or instinctive conditions.

There are consequently four " Elements," *viz.* :—

1. Earth, representing primordial matter, an invisible ethereal substance, forming the basis of all external corporal appearances.

2. Water, referring to the realm of the Soul, the connecting link between spirit and matter. It also represents Thought.

3. Fire, representing the realm of the Spirit or Life.

Astrologically considered fire is an internal activity whose external manifestations are heat and light. This activity differs in character according to the plane on which it manifests itself. " Fire " on the spiritual plane represents Love or Hate; on the astral plane it represents Desire and Passion ; on the physical plane, Combustion. It is the purifying element, and in a certain aspect is identical with " Life."

4. Air, alluding to Space or Form, is not, strictly speaking, an " Element." Space in its various aspects represents the Firmament, the physical and mental horizon, that which limits the physical or mental perception. The sky. The ambient, etc.

There is a fifth element, which is the spiritual quintessence (Mercury among the planets) of all things. Each element may be considered from a variety of aspects.

THE ELEMENTS OF THE ZODIAC

FIRE	△	Transmutable and ascending	— *Length*
EARTH	□	Solid and stationary	— *Thickness*
AIR	=	Flexible and level	— (*4th Dimension*)
WATER	▽	Fluidic and descending	— *Breadth*

Each element constitutes a world of its own, with its own inhabitants, the " elementary spirits of nature " ; and by a combination of elements under various conditions, an endless variety of forms is produced.

The zodiacal elements should not be confounded with the chemical elements. The zodiacal elements are universal and to us invisible principles, the causes of all visible phenomena, whether they are of an earthy (solid), watery (liquid), airy (gaseous), or fiery (ethereal) nature.

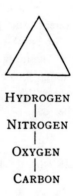

HYDROGEN
|
NITROGEN
|
OXYGEN
|
CARBON

CHAPTER V.

The Planetary Symbols

THE symbols of the planets are simpler than those of the zodiacal signs, being a combination of the Circle, the Semi-Circle and the Cross. According to the arrangement of these symbols, the nature of the planets' influence is revealed.

Spirit, life, consciousness and expansion are denoted by the CIRCLE.

If it is under the Cross, spirit is represented as limited by matter, the Cross being the symbol of restriction and bondage in matter. When the circle is over the Cross, spirit is represented as practically free from the denseness and limitation of matter; not wholly free, but comparatively disentangled.

The SEMICIRCLE denotes the relationship between Circle and Cross; it is neither wholly spirit nor wholly matter, but a compound of the two, and in Esoteric Astrology the Semicircle is the symbol of the Soul.

THE SYMBOLS OF THE PLANETS

Symbol	Planet	Representing	
☉	SUN	Spirit, power	
☽	MOON	Soul, receptivity	1st triad
+	EARTH	Body, definiteness	
☿	MERCURY (*Spiritual Soul*)	Wisdom	
♀	VENUS (*Human Soul*)	Beauty	2nd triad
♂	MARS (*Animal Soul*)	Strength	
♃	JUPITER	Mercy	
♄	SATURN	Justice	3rd triad
♅	URANUS	Will	
♆	NEPTUNE	Submission	Neutral

The Universe as a whole is threefold ; everything exists by ternaries, and Three is the number of manifestation. Every conceivable thing consists of Matter and Motion in Space, and the Three are forever one and inseparable. "God" is a Trinity, and the Universe being a manifestation of God, every part of the Universe must necessarily be threefold. Everything is a product of of thought, will and substance (form).

☉   THE SUN in the highest sense is the symbol of Spirit, the centre of Power, the Heart of things. The Sun is the source of energy and the store-house of power. Each being contains within itself a centre of life, which may grow to be a sun. In the heart of the regenerated man the divine power, stimulated by the Light of the Logos, grows into a Sun which illuminates his mind.

(1) The spiritual Sun of Grace. The Logos or Christ.

Grace is a spiritual power emanating from the Logos ; it should not be confounded with 'favour' or 'partiality.' It is a spiritual influence comparable to the light of the Sun, which shines everywhere, but for which not all things are equally receptive.

Astrologers view the Sun in the heavens as the outward glory of the Solar Logos ; a reflection of the eternal omnipresent self-existent Cause of all things, in its aspect as the Cause of all Good. The meaning of the term " God " differs according to the standpoint from which we view it ; but in its highest meaning it is necessarily beyond the intellectual comprehension of imperfect man ; because the imperfect cannot conceive the perfect, nor the finite the infinite. In one aspect everything that exists is God, and nothing can possibly exist which is not God ; for He is the One Life in which every being has its life and existence. God is the only eternal Reality, unknowable to man ; all that we know of Him are His manifestations.

In one aspect God is looked upon as the spiritual central Sun of the Cosmos, whose rays and substance penetrate the universe with life, light and power. God, in the highest metaphysical sense, being the Absolute cannot have any conceivable relative attributes ; because as nothing exists but Himself, He stands in relation to nothing and is therefore nonexistent from a *relative* point of view. We cannot possibly form any conception of the unmanifested Absolute. But as soon as the latter becomes manifest it appears as a trinity of Thought, Word, and Revelation, *i.e.* as the "Father," the "Son" and the "Holy Ghost."

Innumerable people have been killed because they differed in regard to their opinions of how the term "God" should be defined; but it is (or should be) obvious that a Cause which is beyond all human conception is also beyond any possible correct definition, and that all theological disputations about the nature of God are therefore absurd and useless.

(2) The natural Sun. The centre of all powers contained in our Solar System.

Astrologers consider the terrestrial sun to be the image or reflection of the invisible celestial sun; the latter is in the realm of Spirit what the former is in the realm of Matter; but the material receives its powers from the Spiritual.

☿ MERCURY, semicircle over circle over cross, represents the complete union of the three symbols in one, denoting perfectibility.

♀ VENUS is the symbol of Spirit triumphant over matter, circle over cross. It represents beauty, grace, refinement and all that expresses the *human* state.

♂ MARS, really the cross over the circle, ♂, is the

symbol of spirit constrained by matter. It represents strength, force, physical energy and the animal in man —the animal-man state.

♃ JUPITER, the semicircle rising over the cross, is the symbol of soul liberating itself from matter. It represents mercy, expansion and sympathy.

♄ SATURN, the cross over the semicircle, is the symbol of the soul bound by the form; it represents justice, restraint and definiteness.

♅ URANUS symbolises the unity of the three symbols on a higher grade than Mercury, of which it is the higher octave. It represents will, or the control and abnegation of desire.

♆ NEPTUNE symbolises diversity, or the Many as against the One. It represents submission to authority, divine or otherwise.

Each planet represents a principle, a state of consciousness, or a vibration which can only be responded to by those who have transcended the grosser forms of matter.

Each planet also represents a colour, sound and number—the numbers, however, are always interchangeable.

The seven planets represent the seven principles in man. The real man is an invisible internal and spiritual power which, in its outward manifestation, appears as a human being.

From an astrological standpoint man may be looked upon as an individual ray emanating from the Great Spiritual Sun of the universe, which, having become polarised in the heart of the incipient human organism, endows the latter with life and stimulates its growth. At a certain state of its development that organism becomes conscious of its existence in the phenomenal world, and with this the illusion of *self* is created. There is nothing real and permanent about the being called Man, except this internal divine power which is called the Spirit, and this is ultimately identical with the universal Spirit—the Christ.

PLANETARY TABLE

Planet	Symbol	Colour	Sound	Metal	Character or Expression
SUN	☉	Orange	*Re*	Gold	LIFE—SPIRIT
MOON	☽	Violet	*Si*	Silver	FORM—SOUL
MERCURY	☿	Yellow	*Mi*	Quicksilver	SPIRTUAL SOUL
VENUS	♀	Indigo	*La*	Copper	HUMAN SOUL
MARS	♂	Red	*Do*	Iron	ANIMAL SOUL
JUPITER	♃	Blue	*Sol*	Tin	EXPANSION
SATURN	♄	Green	*Fa*	Lead	CONTRACTION

URANUS is a planet denoting a higher octave of the seven principles, and we may consider it as THE WILL OF THE SELF.

WILL may be said to be the one universal and fundamental power in the universe, from which all other powers take their origin. Fundamentally it is identical with life. It manifests itself in the lower planes of existence as Attraction, Gravitation, Cohesion: on the higher planes as Life, Will, Spiritual Power, etc., according to the conditions in which it acts. The Will is a function of the universal Spirit of God, and there is no other power in the universe but the Will of God, acting either self-consciously, sub-consciously or super-consciously, naturally or spiritually. Man can have no will of his own; he is merely enabled to employ the powers of the universal will acting in his organisation during his earthly existence, and to pervert and misuse them on account of his ignorance of the external laws of nature.

Those who *respond* to the influences of Uranus are sincere observers of human nature, also keen students of occultism, the science of things which transcend the ordinary powers of observation and the perception of which requires extraordinary or super-normal faculties.

Everything is "occult" to us so long as we cannot see it, and with every enlargement of the field of our perception a new and heretofore *occult* world becomes open to our investigation. We may speculate about the Unseen; but we cannot actually know anything about it unless we can mentally grasp its spirit.

By esoteric astrologers Uranus is considered to be the higher octave of Mercury, which in its human expression is the principle of knowledge; in its highest or super-human aspect Mercury represents Wisdom. Knowledge is science based upon the perception and understanding of a truth. Wisdom is the highest conceivable attribute of the spirit; conceivable—like all other powers—only by him in whom wisdom has become manifest, and who is thereby rendered wise. Wisdom is not of man's making; he cannot invent it, but he can acquire it. The same may be said of all other spiritual powers; they exist in the Universe, and are to be attained by man.

NEPTUNE is supposed by esoteric astrologers to be the higher octave of the planet Venus, and represents the highest form of the expression of love, or what we may term Spiritual Love, which is an all-penetrating spiritual power, uniting the higher elements of Humanity into one inseparable whole. It is not led by external sensuous attractions. It is the power by which man recognises the unity of the All, and the product of that knowledge which springs into existence when man recognises the indentity of his own spirit with the spirit of every other being. This spiritual Love should never be confounded with sexual desire, parental affection, etc., which are merely sentiments, subject to attraction and change.

Astrologically mankind may be compared to the metals, which man is ever seeking to temper within himself. The "metals" of which a man is made and which produce his virtues or vices are more permanent and lasting than the body composed of flesh and blood.

CHAPTER VI.

THE SYMBOL OF THE HOROSCOPE

THE horoscope is built up upon the Cross and the Circle, the revolving earth turning upon its axis within a circumscribed area.

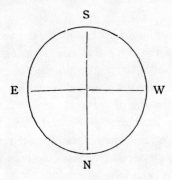

In one complete revolution the whole of the zodiac passes over the meridian, measuring a day of 24 hours.

The midheaven or M.C. is the upper half of the perpendicular line, ending and culminating in the southern point S. The Nadir in the North is designated by N.   The Ascendant denoted by E is in the East, and is the point rising upon the eastern horizon, and the Descendant is in the West, the setting point, W.

(1) Owing to the rotation of the earth on its axis all planets rise in the east and are carried from E to W.

(2) The earth revolves in an orbit round the Sun, and the effect of this is to make the Sun *appear* to move round the earth, passing through the twelve signs of the zodiac in the course of a year of twelve months. When we speak of the "movement" of the Sun, therefore, we use the word in this sense.   This motion, as well as that of the planets in the zodiac, is from W to E.

These two motions of the earth, the rotation on her own axis and the revolution round the Sun, produce a kaleidoscope with an infinite number of patterns, each pattern never repeated in an individual horoscope within a cycle of thousands of years.

The Cross, representing the earth and the physical body of man, is therefore constantly both rotating on its axis and revolving round the sun and thus changing its relationship to everything around it.

The Circle is representative of the atmosphere and the ethers of space around the earth, as well as of the aura around each individual.   If we could see the earth from a distance we should perceive the atmosphere around the earth as a huge globe of ether moving with it.   If we could see our own aura we should appear to be moving enveloped in an egg-shaped sphere of ether. The framework of the horoscope, built up of the rotating cross within the circle, entails definite cycles of change; one takes place every two hours, during which time a complete zodiacal sign passes across the meridian; and another takes place every four minutes, during which time a degree crosses the meridian.

Time is merely succession, and implies motion within a limited area of space. Outside the circle of the earth's atmosphere, or aura, is the much larger circle of the Solar System, the pathway of the Sun and planets termed the Zodiac.

The Ecliptic is identical with the circle of the zodiac, and is divided into twelve equal parts known as the Signs of the Zodiac.[1]

The Celestial Equator is a circle which divides the heavens into northern and southern hemispheres. The circles of the Ecliptic and the Equator do not coincide, but are inclined to each other at an angle of about $23\frac{1}{2}$ degrees.

---

[1] The Zodiac includes the orbits of all the planets, and as these are inclined to the orbit of the Earth at various angles, it is really rather more like a belt than a circle; the Ecliptic is the path of the Sun and lies just in the middle of this belt, deriving its name from the fact that *eclipses* can only happen when the Moon is on, or very close to, this line. For our present purpose, therefore, the zodiac and the ecliptic may be regarded as identical.

The Equator and the Ecliptic are most easily understood with the help of a celestial globe. We may also
get some idea of the astronomical basis of Astrology by
picturing to ourselves an exceedingly large globe, rotating
on its axis in space, and in the centre of it our earth like
a tiny marble. Upon this large globe two circles may
be imagined, crossing each other at an angle of 23½
degrees.

These two circles would represent the Equator and
the Ecliptic: and the points where they cross each other
represent the spring and autumnal equinoxes.

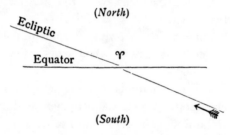

The arrow shows the direction of the sun's movement
along the Ecliptic. Where the sign ♈ is placed is the
point reached by the Sun about March 21st each year
(vernal equinox).

The circle representing the Ecliptic is divided into
twelve parts, known as the Signs of the Zodiac. The
ecliptic itself is a line showing the path of the Sun; and
the zodiac as already explained is a belt, extending to

about 8 degrees on each side of this line, in which all the planets appear to move.   The earth, which we imagine as in the centre of this great globe, is turning on its own axis from west to east and on account of this motion the heavens appear to be moving from east to west.

CHAPTER VII.

THE ZODIAC AND THE HOROSCOPE

THE Cross within the circle may be read as the earth within the zodiac, represented by the eastward-turning

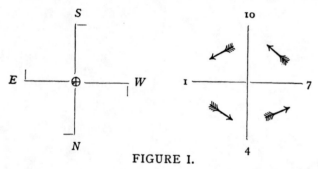

FIGURE I.

swastica (Fig. i.). This is the real motion of rotation of the earth on its axis from west to east; but if, instead of this, attention is concentrated on the heavenly bodies, they of course appear to move round the earth in the opposite direction, from east to west (Fig. ii.). Here the westward-turning swastica represents the direction in which the heavenly bodies appear to rise and set. They rise in the east at the ascendant or first house, pass to the south point or tenth house or mid-heaven, then travel to the west point or descendant or seventh house, thence below the earth to the north point or fourth house, and from there to the east again.

This distinction between the eastward rotation of the earth and the apparent westward motion of the heavenly bodies in their rising and setting should not be forgotten ;

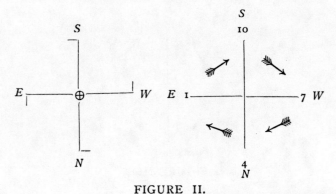

FIGURE II.

it is really very simple, and yet beginners often find themselves confused with it at first.

Substituting the Cardinal signs of the zodiac for $E, S,$ $W,$ and $N,$ we use the symbols ♈ ♑ ♎ ♋.   Taking them in the order of the circle of the zodiac, which is according to the rotation of the Cross or earth, the signs would be arranged as in Fig. iii.   The angles of the horoscope and the Cardinal signs of the zodiac have the same value (Fig. iv.).

The signs and houses that are not cardinal support the angles, and, from the standpoint of a horoscope, they represent the two-hour periods before and after the cardinal houses. The two hours before sunrise and the two hours after support the sunrise; two hours before noon and the two hours after support the noon; two

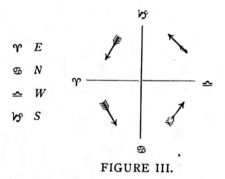

FIGURE III.

hours before sunset and two hours after support the sunset; and two hours before midnight, and two hours after support the midnight.

It is the same with regard to the seasons; the month before spring and the month after support the spring, and so on.

The positions of the supporting signs and houses are marked by the various positions of the compass :—1st house *East*, 2nd *East North East*, 3rd *North North East*, 4th *North*, 5th *North North West*, 6th *W N W*, 7th *West*, 8th *W S W*, 9th *S S W*, 10th *South*, 11th *S S E*, 12th *E S E*.

Each division, house or sign has its own value, but none are so powerful or pronounced as the Angles (1st, 4th, 7th, 10th), and the Cardinal signs (♈, ♋, ♎, ♑)

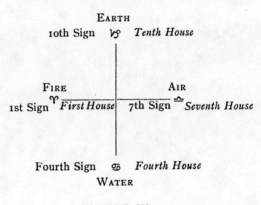

FIGURE IV.

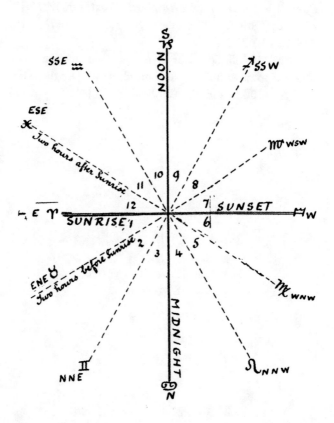

CHAPTER VIII.

SYMBOLICAL HOUSE DIVISIONS

EACH house division of a horoscope has a permanent value and a definite symbolism.

The First house or the Ascendant, as it is termed, represents the Self or the " I am I " centre of consciousness. Just as the rising of the Sun brings daybreak, so the first house symbolises the Self of the person born at any time.

The type of Self is denoted by the *sign* rising at birth which shows the quality of brain, as follows :—

A CARDINAL sign rising, an active brain ; a FIXED sign rising, a slow moving but inflexible brain ; a MUTABLE sign rising, a more flexible and versatile brain.

The disposition and general character of the Self are shown by the planet ruling the rising sign, its position, aspects and so on. The meaning of the term aspects is explained in Chapter XII.

The quality of the influence of the self is shown by the planets rising in the ascendant at the time of birth, with their strengths and weaknesses, etc. Also by aspects to the ascendant received from other planets.

The Angles and the CARDINAL signs correspond to the physical body and all external and manifested activities, and they bring fame, recognition and changes ; they symbolise the *head* of the Self.

The Succedent Houses and the FIXED Signs, which come next in order to the angles and cardinal signs, correspond to the soul, with the feelings, sensations and emotions; they symbolise the *heart* of the Self.

The Cadent Houses and the MUTABLE signs, which come third in order, correspond to the mind, thought and the unseen workings of consciousness; they symbolise the *spirit* of the Self.

Each angle of the horoscope is supported by the succedent and cadent houses and is directly related to them. The second and the twelfth houses support the first ; the ninth and the eleventh houses support the tenth ; the eighth and the sixth houses support the seventh ; and the fifth and the third houses support the fourth.

They are, in *Natal* Astrology, an extension of the angles, and are only divided for particularisation.

The head, brain, and external activities of the Self, shown by the Ascendant, obtain succour and support from the second house and the twelfth.

The life, avocation and honour of the Self, as shown

by the Tenth House, obtain succour and support from the eleventh and ninth houses.

The unions, partnerships and the oppositions to the Self, as shown by the Seventh House, are succoured and supported by the eighth and sixth houses.

The origin, heredity and home life or environment of the Self, as shown by the Fourth House, are supported by the fifth and third houses.

Each house has a rule over certain parts of the physical body as a whole and the houses govern the parts of the body in the same manner as the signs. For the house divisions of a horoscope are a reflection of the zodiacal signs and correspond to them, although on a lower level ; the first sign Aries to the first house, the second sign Taurus to the second house, and so on.

The Sun and planets represent the spiritual consciousness in the heaven world ; the signs of the zodiac represent the astral or psychic consciousness ; and the houses of the horoscope as a whole, represent the physical consciousness. The three kinds of houses correspond as follows :

CADENT HOUSES, III., IX., VI., XII.—Spiritual Consciousness.

SUCCEDENT HOUSES, II., VIII., V., XI.—Psychic Consciousness.

ANGULAR HOUSES, I., VII., X., IV.—Physical Consciousness.

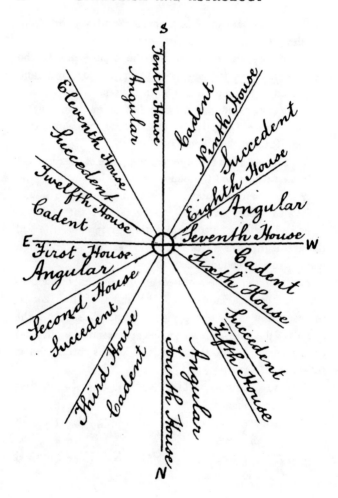

CHAPTER IX.

THE HOUSE DIVISIONS EXPLAINED

EACH house has a special signification with regard to its influence and symbol. The first house usually appears to be the most important, because it is the first channel of outward expression; but in a few cases the tenth house is the strongest in the horoscope because it is the summit of the perpendicular line of power. They are equally important when considered as representative of life and form.

The life manifests as birth and death in the first and seventh houses, the Eastern and Western angles.

The form manifests as objective and subjective expressions of life in the fourth and tenth houses, the Northern and Southern angles.

The ordinary interpretation of the twelve houses has a definite relation to the particulars of life. They are very fully explained in Chapter XV of *Practical Astrology*.

The symbolism of the groups of three houses at the angles reveals their inner meaning.

Each house diminishes or strengthens one of the

angles and the twelve houses act four times as a trinity starting from the angles in the following order:—I, II, XII; X, XI, IX; VII, VIII, VI; IV, V, III.

First	*House*	—	Self-Expression.
Second	„	—	Self-Centredness and Possessions.
Twelfth	„	—	Self-surrender.
Tenth	*House*	—	Honour, Merit, Superiority.
Eleventh	„	—	Social Qualities.
Ninth	„	—	Aspirations.
Seventh House		—	Unions, Equality, Balance.
Eighth	„	—	Separations.
Sixth	„	—	Mental Union.
Fourth House		—	Environment.
Fifth	„	—	Generation.
Third	„	—	Mental Creation.

The FIRST HOUSE, the Self or separate expression of " I am I "; the second house, his possessions, worldly or otherwise; the twelfth house, his charity or benevolence, or the power to sell all he has.

This trinity is either a concrete expression of the forth-going, blind, material self, or the higher expression of the Ego working through that self.

When the interpretation is in terms of the form or selfish animal man, there is more activity in the second house, through the accumulation of possessions, worldly or otherwise, for possession covers all that the native possesses including vice and virtue.

When the life, or human consciousness, is more active than the form, then the twelfth house shows the giving away of possessions, the self-surrender of the form and the activity of the spirit.

The symbolism of the TENTH HOUSE, assisted by the eleventh and the ninth, denotes the moral nature of the Self and its honourable expression through responsibility in the tenth, the collection of many friends and social welfare through the eleventh, and the prayers and aspirations through religion or philosophy shown by the ninth house.

In a worldly and material application the tenth would denote reputation or notoriety, the eleventh acquaintances and conventions, and the ninth orthodoxy and pretentions.

The symbolism of the SEVENTH HOUSE, the western angle, with the eighth and sixth houses, denotes the union of the Self with other Selves ; the realisation of unity and brotherhood.

The eighth denotes the dissolution of physical or concrete ties, and a wider expansion of consciousness ; the sixth, the proper relationship to inferiors, or those who co-operate for the common good, also the complete subjugation of the physical body.

In an undeveloped horoscope the seventh shows physical marriage and sex unions, the eighth deaths, and the sixth shows work and labour and servitude and bondage to the physical.

The symbolism of the FOURTH HOUSE, with its

supporters the fifth and third, has a psychic interpretation, revealing the inner and more silent manifestation of the Self.

The fourth house shows the state at the end of physical life, the fifth the powers of generation, the multiplication of forms, and the third the creative powers of the mind. In the undeveloped horoscope the fourth shows the heredity, the fifth the gratification of the physical self, and the third mental pleasures, journeys, and brethren of the family.

Each house is pregnant with meaning and yields many interpretations. The horoscope as a whole describes the destiny; and the twelve houses, although considered separately here, really interact and modify each other. Any house can affect and modify any other in an important manner, and they do this through the ever varying planetary positions in their relationship to the zodiacal signs.

CHAPTER X.

The Nature of the Zodiacal Signs

THE twelve signs of the zodiac symbolise the various conditions of etheric matter surrounding our globe ; they represent certain well defined states of this finest etheric substance. Modern Astrologers know these states as *Fixed*—AIR, FIRE, WATER, and EARTH ; *Cardinal*—AIR, FIRE, WATER, and EARTH ; *Mutable*—AIR, FIRE, WATER, and EARTH.[1] The highest and most subtle form of Ether may be said to be a synthesis of all the etheric conditions, although it comes forth in those states that we call fixed, movable[2] and mutable or interchangeable. These conditions of the primary ether are due to certain modes of motion or vibration. They are rotary

---

[1] See Chapter IV.

[2] ' Movable ' and ' cardinal ' as applied to the signs are interchangeable terms.

motion which is Fixed, translatory motion which is
Cardinal, and vibratory motion which is Mutable; and
these again produce the essence of fire, earth, air and
water, which have some correspondence with the
elements, although they are not identical with them.   It
is from these states of ether that astrologers judge the
temperament of the physical body and the class or
type of body through which the soul is working.   The
sign rising at the birth of an individual shows the
peculiar type of brain the child will possess, and according to the nature of the zodiacal sign so the quality is
judged.

The physical temperament is also considerably
influenced by the type of sign in which the majority of
planets are placed.   Over *each* sign there is a ruling
planet, or to speak more correctly, each planet has
affinity with certain zodiacal signs, the planetary vibrations acting as the spirit or energising influence behind
the sign.

In a general sense, the Sun and the planet Uranus
preside over the FIXED signs; Mercury and Jupiter over
the MUTABLE signs; and the Moon, Saturn and Venus
over the CARDINAL signs.   Saturn has also some affinity
with the *Airy* signs, the Sun with the *Fiery* signs, and
Mars, the Moon and Jupiter with the *Watery* signs;
while all the planets have some influence over the
Earthy signs.

In a particular sense each planet, with the exception of the Sun and Moon, rules over two signs, which are called its *Houses*, as follows, + indicating positive and − negative.

	Planet	Signs	Planet	
+	♄	♒.................♑	♄	−
−	♃	♓...............♐	♃	+
+	♂	♈............♏	♂	−
−	♀	♉.........♎	♀	+
+	☿	♊.......♍	☿	−
−	☽	♋...♌	☉	+

Symbolically therefore, each planet is at the apex of a positive and negative mode of motion, itself remaining neutral so far as these opposite poles are concerned.

Saturn appears to be a negative planet, and its influence seems strongest in the negative sign Capricorn, but it is really neither positive nor negative; it can be translated into either according to the use that is made of the vibration.

The influence of Saturn in the atmosphere is such as to produce cold, and in this condition it coincides with an Aquarian effect; but on the earth it produces dampness and moisture, corresponding to Capricorn.

Saturn apart from these signs is the symbol of the universal principle of matter; the producer and destroyer of forms.

There are certain signs in which the planets have a very potent influence, and these are called the *Exaltations* of the planets :—

Exaltation

♄ in ♎ ⎫
♃ „ ♋ ⎪ CARDINAL signs, or signs of action and change.
♂ „ ♑ ⎬
☉ „ ♈ ⎭
♀ „ ♓ MUTABLE.
☽ „ ♉ FIXED.
☿ „ ♍ NEUTRAL ; having the least affinity with the signs.

The planets ☿ ♅ and ♆ are not so restricted to definite signs of the zodiac as are the others.

Each sign symbolises a virtue which may be expressed in general terms as follows :—

THE VIRTUES OF THE SIGNS.

♈	*Self-Sacrifice*	♎	*Harmony*
♉	*Obedience*	♏	*Attachment*
♊	*Reason*	♐	*Hope*
♋	*Sympathy*	♑	*Service*
♌	*Faith*	♒	*Loyalty*
♍	*Discrimination*	♓	*Compassion*

Each has, of course, a corresponding vice which may be said to be the inversion, or the abuse or misuse, of the virtue. The signs of the zodiac are, however, more concerned with the form side of human expression, while the life or consciousness comes under the influence of the planets.

CHAPTER XI.

THE NATURE OF THE PLANETS

THE planets seen in the heavens are the physical centres of great spheres of influence, and around each is a subtle atmosphere which may be said to be the aura of the planet. Within each aura are hosts of celestial beings who obey the Will of the Supreme Intelligence who presides over the sphere.

While Astrology is scientific, tracing the vibrations or influences of the planets to the planet itself, it does not attribute the whole of that influence to the *physical* planet any more than it attributes the whole of the natal influences in a horoscope to the rising sign or ruling planet. Astrology teaches that the Solar System is one complete whole, but made up of an infinite number of parts. It is One great Life over which a great Being called the Solar Logos presides, the God of the System.

The planetary spheres, although appearing separate, are inter-blended and form well-defined but inter-linked parts of the whole. The earth's superphysical atmosphere interblends with that of Venus and the other planets, so that not one of them is actually separate.

It is the same with every kingdom or department of nature ; the mineral kingdom is apparently separate, but mineral matter is found in other kingdoms as well.

Saturn appears to govern and control the mineral kingdom only, but its range of influence really extends from the mineral to the finest grades of ether and beyond ; for it is the principle that gives the power of resistance to everything in manifestation. Saturn may, therefore, govern the gigantic rock or mountain, the sturdy oak or rigid tree, and the bones in the animal creature ; but the same influence also gives gravity to the character, faithfulness to the emotions, and concentration to the mind. As with Saturn so with every planet. The angels or Shining Ones who work unseen to human sight, fashioning all things into perfect shape and beauty of form, work together as a whole.

Man makes distinctions and views all things as separate, and this is useful for the purpose of clearing his ideas, but it is we who are causing the separation which seems so real, whereas, it is apparent only.

There is in every human being a correspondence with the planetary spheres, and hence the possibility of man's *response* to planetary vibrations. The physical body is a complete whole, yet is at the same time divisible into many parts, and to each part the correspondence may be traced : —

The bony structure to SATURN
The blood and the cells to JUPITER
The muscular system to MARS
The flesh and tissues to VENUS
The nervous system to MERCURY
The nervous fluids to URANUS
The life and vitality to the SUN
The etheric body to the MOON

From the physical body to the soul, and thence to the spirit, there is a continuous correspondence, which makes man's immortal link with the Divine.

The rigidity of Saturn does not apply to the bones alone, but to the self-reliance of the soul and the patience of the spirit.

The fluidity of the blood, the growth and adaptability of the cellular system, are not only physical, but through Jupiter the soul is sympathetic, benevolent and merciful, and the spirit compassionate. Jupiter is the seed planet, representing a germ, an element, or a power from which a being may grow; " Jupiter " is therefore in the minerals, plants, animals and man, as well as in the heavens.

The influence of Mars does not stop at the muscular system; it strengthens the soul, and through courage and heroism tends to the devotion of the spirit. The rule of Venus over the flesh and symmetry of form is extended to the beauty of the soul and the grace of the spirit.

The nervous system under Mercury, although affording the lines of communication for physical response to internal and external stimuli, gives adaptability to the soul, and leads to the intuition of the spirit.

The nervous fluids, although electrified by Uranus, have also a link with the soul through its inward expansion, which eventually leads to the Will of the Spirit.

The vitality of the body, which is an impregnation from the Sun, is also the life of the soul and the consciousness of the spirit.

Astrology teaches "as above so below." Everything in Nature is directly or indirectly affected by the vibrations of the planetary spheres.

The make-up of the body is fixed or resistant, cardinal or responsive, and mutable or variable, according to the signs of the zodiac predominating at our birth. The circle contains all, but the Cross divides it into varying parts with different characteristics.

Astrology teaches that the essence of man may be discovered through the divine trinity of Will, Love and Wisdom; for all desire in every shape and form is the polar opposite of Will, and all knowledge, no matter in what shape, is the reflection of Divine Wisdom, and all love, in whatever shape or form, makes towards the divine unity, which is the love of God. For man is in reality a divine being ever striving to express Will, Love and Wisdom, and it is only because he blindly attempts to give expression to his true nature, that in exercising his desires, he makes errors and mistakes that are due to his ignorance. For Astrology teaches that sin is really ignorance, and when man is free through knowledge, he strikes away from the vibrations of desire and learns to use his will in order that he may no longer be the creature of circumstances, held by environment; but instead he learns to make his own circumstances and environment.

Now the synthesis of all the planets is Uranus, just as the synthesis of the zodiacal signs may be expressed through Aquarius, the Man ; for Uranus represents the true individual which has been formed through the ages by the Solar vibrations. The Sun's rays gives out the particles of life which man absorbs into himself, changing that life from the animal expression of force into the mental energy of man-hood until it reaches devotion to the divine, for it is the same life which permeates all things and the more of this life man can absorb and use wisely, the more truly individualised does he become, and by setting his will towards the goal, he can by his own individual efforts strive to become more and more like unto his divine prototype.

Now at our present stage of evolution, there are very few who can respond to the high vibrations of Uranus, but this planet, as Astrology teaches, is the goal to which man is ever striving, for it represents the apex of the triangle in which Will, Love and Wisdom are blended.

In our present stage we find man at all stages of evolution ; some trying to respond to martial vibrations, in which courage, and finally heroism is to be expressed, and others trying to respond to Jupiter's influence, through which expansion, sympathy and mercy are finally to be expressed in compassion.

Then again, some are seeking to express the vibrations of Saturn which give perseverance, steadfastness, patience and ultimately truth.   On all sides we see man seeking to temper the influences of the stars within himself, and as these vibrations in their highest aspect are exceedingly difficult to absorb and can only be manifest after many lives in various bodies, it will be seen that Astrology teaches man's evolution from the animal to the God, and since we find it difficult for man to express the highest vibrations of the various planets, it becomes still more difficult to temper the whole of these influences into himself until the Uranian or Neptunian temperament is manifest ; for Uranus represents the occultist and Neptune represents the mystic or true devotee.   In striving to reach the highest, Astrology helps every man by pointing out the way and teaching him to find the principle in himself, and although we have only touched upon the fringe of this vast subject of Astrology it is neither too difficult nor too hard to learn, but may be acquired by all who try to understand their own nature.

CHAPTER XII.

A SYMBOLIC ASPECTARIAN

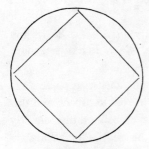 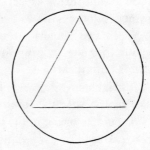

The Angle of Sorrow;
unfortunate.

The Angle of Joy;
fortunate.

THE constantly varying relations between the planets
are summed up and classified by the astrologer under
what are known as Aspects, and these are either good or
evil. Strictly speaking they are neither good nor evil,
but are only forces that are used or abused by man, who
experiences the result in pleasure or pain.

It is true that there is the angle of sorrow and the
angle of joy, but these indicate discord and harmony in

the characters of those who come under them and experience their effects.

Each aspect symbolises a fact in Nature, and each sets up a tension which is either too strong or too relaxed where extremes are concerned. The aspects are simple in their nature, though liable to very complex interpretations.

When two planets are exactly *one* sign apart, they form a semi-sextile aspect, which is slightly good, and is symbolised thus——⊻

When two planets are exactly *one and a half* signs apart, they are in semi-square, which is half a square and is unfortunate——∠.

A neighbourly aspect is formed when two planets are *two* signs apart; they are then in sextile aspect, and this is favourable owing to the influence being either directly positive or directly negative, the sextile being always made from two positive or two negative signs,——✳.

When two planets are *three* signs apart, they are in square aspect, this is the angle of sorrow, and is formed from signs that are not congenial in nature, such as fire and water, earth and air, etc. It is sorrowful, as representing the struggle between the mind and the senses, or reason and sensation. It is symbolised thus——□.

When two planets are *four* signs apart, they are in trine aspect, which is the angle of joy, and is favourable, owing to the signs in which it is formed being in sympathy or in the same triplicity. They may be both fire, or both air, etc. The trine aspect is signified thus —— △

When two planets are exactly *four and a half* signs apart, they are in sesqui-square or sesqui-quadrate; like the semi-square it is unfavourable,—— ⚼

When two planets are *six* signs apart or "in opposition," they are at extreme tension, a condition of stringency—— ☍.

When they are both together in the same sign, they are "in conjunction," or in extreme relaxed tension—— ☌.

The aspects are seen to be simple when related to the signs of the zodiac. The fire, earth, air and water signs are always in square or opposition aspect the one to the other, as follows.

Squares or Oppositions.

♈	♋	♎	♑—CARDINAL
♌	♏	♒	♉—FIXED
♐	♓	♊	♍—MUTABLE

while signs of the same triplicity are always in trine aspect, thus:

Trines.

♈	♌	♐—FIRE
♉	♍	♑—EARTH
♊	♎	♒—AIR
♋	♏	♓—WATER

It is the same with the house-divisions of a horoscope; the angles are always in square to each other, and so are the succedent and the mutable houses. The trines or triangles are the 1st, 5th and 9th, and by adding four signs to any sign as a starting point, the trines are formed, as 2nd, 6th, or 10th; the 3rd, 7th, and 11th; and the 4th, 8th and 12th.

Symbols of Aspects	Distance or Degrees Apart		Nature
♂ CONJUNCTION	Together	0°	Variable
⊻ SEMI-SEXTILE	One sign apart	30°	Slightly good
∠ SEMI-SQUARE	One and a half signs apart	45°	Moderately evil
⚹ SEXTILE	Two signs apart	60°	Good
□ SQUARE	Three signs apart	90°	Very evil
△ TRINE	Four signs apart	120°	Very good
⊡ SESQUI-QUAD-RATE	Four and a half signs apart	135°	Evil
⚻ QUINCUNX	Five and a half signs apart	150°	Variable
☍ OPPOSITION	Six and a half signs apart	180°	Very evil

Symbolically, the aspects repeat the attitude of man toward certain conditions or positions. We experience sorrow when we seek to run counter to Nature's laws. We reach joy when we work harmoniously with Nature. Fire and water are splendid and useful elements in their own sphere, but when they interfere with each other, there is sure to be inharmony.

When we allow the senses to become a playground for the mind, we are trying to make fire and water amalgamate, and when we prostitute the spirit for the benefit of the physical, we are trying to blend the incompatible air and earth.

The secret of joy and sorrow lies in the attitude of our mind toward our surroundings and circumstances, and this is symbolically shown in every horoscope.

It is important to remember that Astrology uses the terms good and evil in a relative sense only; everything conducive to a purpose in view is relatively good; but only that which leads to permanent happiness is permanent Good. Everything, therefore, which ennobles and elevates mankind may be called good, while that which degrades is evil. Supreme good is that which establishes real and permanent happiness.

CHAPTER XIII.

The Individuality and the Personality.

From an esoteric standpoint the Sun is the symbol in every horoscope of what may be termed the Individuality, the more stable and permanent centre of the Self; while the Moon is a symbol of the Personality, that which is changeable and subject to the moods of the mental and psychic parts of the nature. These terms are very useful to the student of Astrology, as they denote the polarity of Spirit and Soul; the Spirit expressing itself as the Individuality, as the moral tone of the character, as the high water mark of the self and its expression. But this should not be taken too literally, since the Sun is only a symbol of the highest manifestation of life, although there is a certain indication in every nativity which shows the general trend of the moral character. For instance, the Sun forming a favourable aspect to the various planets colours or strengthens the individual character according to the nature of the planet with which it is in aspect, and although the nature of the aspect shows the tendency or use which will be made of the moral character, the astrologer has to exercise much care in not laying too much stress upon the aspects apart from the position of the various planets in relation to the Sun. For instance, the Sun in conjunction or in other good aspect with Jupiter expresses itself through the sympathetic nature, tending to evolve a more benevolent, merciful and kind disposition, and eventually producing the ideal virtue of compassion, thus causing the Individuality to express itself along the line of compassion or pure unselfish feeling. Now an adverse aspect of the Sun to Jupiter may tend to make one somewhat hypocritical, or strongly inclined to form and ceremony without being sufficiently sincere, and lacking the ability to express the influence of Jupiter unselfishly. But all aspects between the Sun and Jupiter tend to give expansion and opportunity for the development of the moral and higher side of the character, and as the character evolves upwards with increased knowledge, this influence of Jupiter brings the expansion of mind or wide-mindedness which enables the individual to be tolerant to others. When expressing itself through the feeling side of the nature it exhibits devotion, religious aspiration and an expansion of the sympathies.

Now the aspects of the Sun to Saturn will act in quite a different manner. The Sun in conjunction or benefic aspect to Saturn brings much reserve and restriction, and endows the individual side of the character with great gravity, so that the Saturnian colouring makes the native lay great stress upon duty and causes him to think more of responsibility than would be the case when the Sun aspects Jupiter or any other of the planets.

The highest vibration to which the Saturnian individual can respond will be that which causes him to accentuate all his responsibilities, in order that justice, and ultimately truth, may wholly colour the Individuality.

Those aspects of Saturn to the Sun which are termed adverse tend to harden the nature and make the individual separative, self-centred and inclined to observe only those duties which bring the most recompense and sufficient remuneration to pay for the labour involved. But while Saturn tends to bring restriction, it also gives that power to reason which evolves a very strong Individuality, and makes for patience, truth and purity. All these characteristics of Saturn, tend to make the Individuality powerful and strong on this particular line of development.

The Sun in conjunction or benefic aspect with Mars would strengthen the character, giving much force and determination, which when used for moral development would express itself as righteous indignation, but when used for combating wrong or evil, would produce courage, heroism and all those qualities which tend to bring out

devotion as an ideal; while the adverse aspect of the
Sun to Mars would probably give too much combative-
ness and a tendency to use the force and strength
selfishly, and thus to produce in the Individuality an
element of aggressiveness and destruction. . . . In
this sense it will be seen that the Solar line represents
what may be termed the Individuality in the making,
which becomes stronger and more pronounced as the
virtues of the planets are absorbed and expressed
through the individual side of the character. For while
the Sun may be taken in every horoscope to represent
what we may term the Individual Centre, it only represents
that centre as the nucleus of the moral character, which
is the result of an absorption of vibrations from the more
powerful planets, that have made, as it were, the very
fabric of our nature.

When, however, all the planetary vibrations are
absorbed they return back through the Individuality and
are expressed as character, becoming synthesised in the
planetary vibration of Uranus, which may be said to be
the real planetary symbol of the Individuality, since it
represents the whole nature of man, or the centre of that
which makes him an Individualised Self. But only a
very few can respond to the Uranian vibrations, just as
there are many who have yet to learn to manifest the best
side of Jupiter, Saturn or Mars. Weak individuals are
those who cannot respond to the planetary influences

E

and are therefore not moved from within, but are simply affected by their environment, physical surroundings and conditions (of which they are more or less an echo), and being controlled by them, they repeat them over and over again.   In this sense do we understand the motto of the ancients " The Wise Man rules his Stars, the Fool obeys them."

From an esoteric standpoint the Moon represents the Personality, even as the Sun is the symbol of the Individuality, but it is a symbol only, denoting the characteristics of the various planets as coloured and reflected by the Moon.   In other words, the Moon by her rapid motion translates the vibrations of the various planets, passing on from one to another just as the animal or sensational mind of man moves from one condition to another, constantly changing, without permanence or reliability, expressing at one time one side of his nature, and at another time, another side, and passing through a series of moods every day, that mood being more pronounced which accords with the influence predominating.

Therefore the Moon may be taken as the symbol of the Personality, reflecting the nature of the sign of the zodiac in which it was placed at birth and then receiving the influences of the planets, and translating them in lunar terminology of moods and tenses.

For instance, the Moon in conjunction or in benefic

aspect with Saturn will tend to give a certain personal reserve, a tendency to be strict, circumspect and self-controlled. This may tend to work out as perseverance, industry, patience, and those restraining qualities which make the personality steadfast and more or less thorough and truthful. For all benefic aspects are more readily absorbed along the line of joy while the adverse aspects owing to their nature, tend to produce experiences by the way of sorrow. So the astrologer judges the Personality to be uncontrolled when there are adverse aspects of the Moon to Saturn and when such is the case the person frets and resents the general conditions around him, and instead of trying to understand and make the most of the influences he is passing through, he usually rebels and brings sorrow upon himself, not only through the Saturnian influences to the Moon, but through his attitude towards them.

The conjunction and other favourable aspects of the Moon to Jupiter will give a very hopeful and joyous personality, with the power of taking an optimistic view of things, and of seeing the good in preference to the bad. With the expansion it brings into the Personality there is always a love of social life, of exchanging views and ideas that is generally attractive to others, and produces what is termed a lucky Personality, due wholly to the attitude that is taken towards life and people.

This expansion then brings a philosophic attitude of

mind, a tendency to religious observances and an inclination to look on the bright side of life and overcome the sorrows and difficulties with a lighter heart than those who do not respond to these Jupiterian influences.

The adverse aspects of the Moon to Jupiter make for prodigality, and bring trouble through excess and the inclination to be too free and not sufficiently circumspect or well regulated in life.

The same idea may be traced to the Moon in good aspect with Mars, where the tendency is toward impulse and a general out-rush of feeling with little or no restraint. Used in the right direction this out-rushing feeling makes the Personality responsive and ever ready to spring forward to those who need assistance, whereas the adverse aspects to Mars give a tendency to use these forces along the line of sensation and the indulgence of the senses without sufficient restraint and due recognition of consequences.

The same ideas may be followed with regard to good aspects between the Moon and Venus, which give the love of all beautiful things, and the desire to give pleasure to others; and these influences generally coincide with a personality that is musical or artistic and fond of ministering to the general happiness and well-being of others. But where the aspects are not favourable, the Personality as represented by the Moon and Venus is inclined to be too forward, very indulgent in pleasure, and with a strong tendency to live in the sensational side of the nature rather than in the mind or restrained senses.

From this idea it may be seen that the Personality is only a symbol, represented by the Moon. The aspects of the Moon colour the Personality according to the nature of the planets aspecting the Moon at birth, and gives to it certain inclinations or tendencies, with which the person born at that time more or less identifies himself. When the astrologer studies these from an esoteric standpoint, he considers all the acquired Personal characteristics (especially the more pronounced of them), which will eventually re-act upon the Individual side of the nature, and be finally expressed in the Individual character, which has been built up by the Personality during numbers of lives. Although the Moon is only used figuratively for the Personality, it nevertheless represents that Personality to all intents and purposes; and it is from this that the astrologer gives his judgment with regard to the personal characteristics.

The skilful astrologer blends the position of the Sun and the Moon into what is termed a Polarity, a full description of which has been given in *Astrology for All*, also in the first manual of the whole series, entitled *Everybody's Astrology*.

CHAPTER XIV.

FATE AND FREE WILL.

THE question naturally arises in the mind of those who are interested in Astrology and its practical workings, as to whether the Individuality and the Personality are fated to act in accordance with the planetary vibrations coming from the planets to the Sun and the Moon.

Now the Esoteric Astrologer is by no means a fatalist, for he believes that every man has by his past thoughts, feelings and actions produced a certain vibration within himself which tends to express the whole of the character in certain directions; therefore, the Esoteric Astrologer believes in the soul's re-embodiment, and considers that every man brings into the present life the results of his past thoughts, feelings and actions, as character. There is, however, a far more subtle and deeper meaning with regard to fate than the soul's previous conditions or attitude towards manifest life. The vehicles and bodies through which the spirit and soul are working are represented by the signs of the Zodiac, and the houses of the horoscope may be taken as fated to express themselves in that particular way, for the bodies are made up of matter tending to vibrate

70

in certain directions, each body being more or less attuned to act in accordance with the impetus given in the past.

It is the nature of Aries to produce an impulsive character, and the nature of Capricorn to produce a restrained one ; so that the body built up more by Aries than by Capricorn would be more or less impulsive and rash, whereas the person born under Capricorn or where the Capricornian influence was pronounced, would be more restrained and less inclined to act thoughtlessly or rashly.

The Astrologer believes that man is fated to live according to his vehicles, or it may be said according to the temperament of his body, which is really the result of the tempering of all the influences of the various planets and zodiacal signs in the past. When man realises that it is only the vehicles which tend to act in certain directions and that he, the spirit, is Lord or master over the vehicles, he will be able to exhibit free will.

Therefore man is free to think for himself, but he cannot think individually if his thought has been coloured by the impressions of others or by a too strong heredity or early environment. The strong individual thinks independently and seeks to know the right from the wrong, the true from the false, the life from the form ; so that in this respect we may say knowledge

brings freedom, whereas ignorance or non-knowledge
brings bondage. The man who is bound by his vehicles
or the form through which his spirit is manifesting, is
what the Astrologer would term "the fool who obeys
his stars," whereas the man who seeks to refine his
body by pure living and right action, gradually conquers
the matter of his vehicles and dominates them and
makes them servants to his will, thus becoming the
"wise man who rules his stars."

It is impossible to explain fully the relationship that
exists between Astrology and fate and free will, in a
small manual of this kind. It may be remarked,
however, that in the composition of every being there
are metals which are of the same nature as the metals
in the stars; there is also an aura surrounding the
vehicles of every man, the colours of which are
identical with the colours in the stars; and indeed
there are also tones and over tones within the human
principles, so that each man sounds the particular chord
of his being which is more or less in harmony with the
music of the spheres.

It is because man the microcosm is made in the
image of the macrocosm that he comes under the
influence of the stars, for man was made in the image
of God. The whole Universe is God, and man is part
of that Universe, and when he learns to co-operate with
the higher spheres he then truly becomes a Son of God.

CONCLUSION

ASTROLOGY as a science teaches the relationship of the part to the whole. It defines both ; the WHOLE as the Solar System with a mighty spiritual Intelligence at the centre, the PART as the great spiritual Beings who work with the Logos or God of the System as the Divine part or parts who carry out his will.

Astrology as an art shows the philosophy of the Whole and the purpose of the Parts.

Astrology is simple in its teachings of the Unity ; it is complex in its interpretation of the Multiplicity.

From an esoteric standpoint Astrology demonstrates the idea that CHARACTER IS DESTINY, and shows how man is freed by knowledge and enabled to overcome the limitations of matter.

It shows how man is fated by the nature and quality of the vehicles through which he, as a spirit or Divine fragment, is working, and how he may spin the web of destiny that will constitute his future horoscope by improving his character.

It reiterates with greater force than ever the ancient motto—"*The wise man rules his stars, the fool obeys them.*"

It explains the nature of fate and shows wherein lies free-will.

It seeks to understand the particular fate of each man or woman, and points out the remedy—knowledge.

Each horoscope is shown to be a chart of the Self, whether the higher self or the lower does not matter for the present; in either case it accurately describes the kind of physical body in which the soul is clothed.

It shows the *tendencies* of the soul, and how the spirit may be unfolded along the lines of least resistance.

A TIME FOR EVERYTHING

From birth to death in the physical world we are plunged into a series of varied activities, all of which we relate to the terms past, present and future.

The earth's revolution on her axis causes relative time to be divided into years, months, weeks, days, and smaller periods. It is said that the entire fabric of Hindu Astrology rests upon the broad principles of evolution in time, and it would seem from a materialistic standpoint that Astrology is a science mainly concerned with Time and Space.

From vast cycles embracing great world periods to the passing moment, there is a purpose in the divisions of time, and those who study Astrology deeply cannot fail to be convinced that there is a time for everything and a purpose in everything connected with life embodied in form.

The whole subject of time is a vital one, wherever Astrology is concerned, and its study is based upon the exact science of mathematics. As an example we may take the circle of the zodiac which is a unity and a complete whole divisible into a series of parts. For instance, the circle and its subdivision produces a series to which a known value has been attached ; we not only produce triangles, quadrants, circles, and other definite measurements, but also definitely state their numerical value and attach a specific quality to each.

No matter how serious the blunders and ignorance of its professors and interpreters may be, the study of Astrology is founded upon the exact sciences, and is capable of yielding results that are eminently satisfactory when considered by the careful and painstaking student.

Just as there is a purpose in everything, so there is a time for everything. We are all born at a certain time, at a certain place, and of parents who were also born under certain definite conditions. Has the particular hour of our birth any special meaning ? Astrologers for ages and in all parts of the world have studied the hour of birth and written horoscopes with an assurance that is either mere presumption, or else is based upon a knowledge that is unimpeachable. That a large number of mountebanks exist who pretend to a knowledge they do not possess is undeniable; but that fact does not preclude an individual study of the subject by those who are thoughtful and interested in matters that pertain to time and space.

To any who are doubtful concerning the statement that the foundations of Astrology are based upon the exact sciences, the general idea of the subject may be illustrated by the divisibility of the zodiacal circle, provided the established value of ancient symbolism is recognised as a species of abstract mathematics.

The circle of the zodiac as a homogeneous whole is a unit symbolising the number 1. It belongs to a plane or sphere where the symbols of concrete manifestations begin.

It represents the synthesis or primordial basis of matter, homogeneous and essential, and for this reason it has been termed the "Circle of Necessity" or "The Wheel of Destiny."

Astrology is not a new science, it is the most ancient of which the world is aware. It has been interpreted by men of all ages and in every land through the same symbology that was first given to men by Divine teachers.

Its rules are the same for all, and those rules are as simple as they can be, and moreover there is no man or woman of ordinary intelligence who cannot understand them.

In this small book, however, only a brief sketch has been given of its main principles.

Previous to the publication of this Manual, No. 1 of a New Series, fourteen manuals have been issued, giving the rules for making a thorough study of the subject. They are written in simple language with a view to teaching those who are willing to learn. To cast a horoscope and learn how to judge it *What is a Horoscope and How is it Cast* is strongly recommended.

To those who wish to be convinced before they study, *Astrology for All* will speedily bring that conviction; and to those who would judge the whole horoscope without the trouble of casting it, *The Key To Your Own Nativity* is recommended: it gives a series of ready-made judgments suitable to the normal individual who is moving with the tide of evolution without making special efforts towards progress.

The present manual has been written more particularly

as an Introduction to the subject of Astrology, and those who wish to carry the ideas further may do so by studying the author's latest work, *Esoteric Astrology*.

Further details concerning the earlier manuals and books will be found in the following pages, also particulars of the Correspondence Lessons, monthly magazine, etc., etc.

COSIMO is an innovative publisher of books and publications that inspire, inform and engage readers worldwide. Our titles are drawn from a range of subjects including health, business, philosophy, history, science and sacred texts. We specialize in using print-on-demand technology (POD), making it possible to publish books for both general and specialized audiences and to keep books in print indefinitely. With POD technology new titles can reach their audiences faster and more efficiently than with traditional publishing.

> ➢ **Permanent Availability:** Our books & publications never go out-of-print.

> ➢ **Global Availability:** Our books are always available online at popular retailers and can be ordered from your favorite local bookstore.

COSIMO CLASSICS brings to life unique, rare, out-of-print classics representing subjects as diverse as *Alternative Health, Business and Economics, Eastern Philosophy, Personal Growth, Mythology, Philosophy, Sacred Texts, Science, Spirituality* and much more!

COSIMO-on-DEMAND publishes your books, publications and reports. If you are an Author, part of an Organization, or a Benefactor with a publishing project and would like to bring books back into print, publish new books fast and effectively, would like your publications, books, training guides, and conference reports to be made available to your members and wider audiences around the world, we can assist you with your publishing needs.

Visit our website at www.cosimobooks.com to learn more about Cosimo, browse our catalog, take part in surveys or campaigns, and sign-up for our newsletter.

And if you wish please drop us a line at info@cosimobooks.com. We look forward to hearing from you.

Printed in the United States
119931LV00001B/37/A

9 781596 056145